A YEAR OF *adventure!*

Toby has a Dream

Book-3

Written by David Bannister ©
Illustrated by Kathryn Bannister ©

The Gate is left open

Toby was having a good old snooze. He was having such a deep sleep you could hear him snoring.

Toby started to dream of days when he was a pup growing up.

Mr & Mrs Brown lived next door and they had one little boy called Jackson. Jackson had moved to year 3 and was finding the schoolwork hard.

One bright spring evening Jackson was planning to go out into the garden to play ball. He usually did this after school.

Today was going to be different.

Mum had just gone upstairs to check if the bedrooms were tidy.

Jackson had left his room in a mess.

He was supposed to be doing his spelling homework.

Mum went in to check on him and was cross when she saw the mess of his room.

After Jackson's Mum had noticed his room was in a mess she took a look at his Homework book. She was disappointed there were no spellings written down.

Jackson complained that they were too hard.

He had ten spellings to learn for his homework.

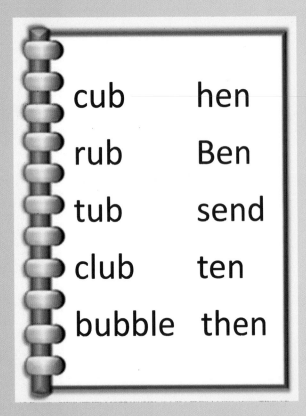

cub	hen
rub	Ben
tub	send
club	ten
bubble	then

Mum said he had to tidy his room and have his homework finished before Dad came home.

Dad arrived home from a busy day in the office. Mum called Jackson to see dad.

Dad suddenly said "Shhhh" as he set a cardboard box down, ever so carefully, at his feet.

Jackson looked at the box as it seemed to be swelling and moving by itself.

Jackson asked dad what was inside the box.

Dad said it was a surprise.

Dad told Jackson to put his hand in the box and guess what was inside. Jackson reached in but pulled his hand back quickly.

Dad laughed and Jackson tried again.

This time he got licked by something which made him pull his hand away for the second time.

Jackson tried a third time and this time he grabbed what it was. To his surprise it was a puppy Samoyed!

Jackson had a great big smile across his face when dad told

him the puppy was

for him.

Jackson called his new

pup Toby.

Dad said that Jackson could go out to play in the garden with Toby if his homework was done and his bedroom was tidy.

Mum and Jackson knew that there was still work to be done.

Jackson went to his room to see if he could finish his homework and tidy up his toys.

Toby sat down on the floor and Jackson sat at his desk learning his spellings.

"These are hard," said Jackson.

"No, they're not." said Toby.

"Who said that?" asked Jackson as he looked around his room. "It was me," said Toby.

"You can talk!" said Jackson.

"To learn your spellings," said Toby, "have a good look at them, cover them and write them down. Then check to see if you're right and do it again".

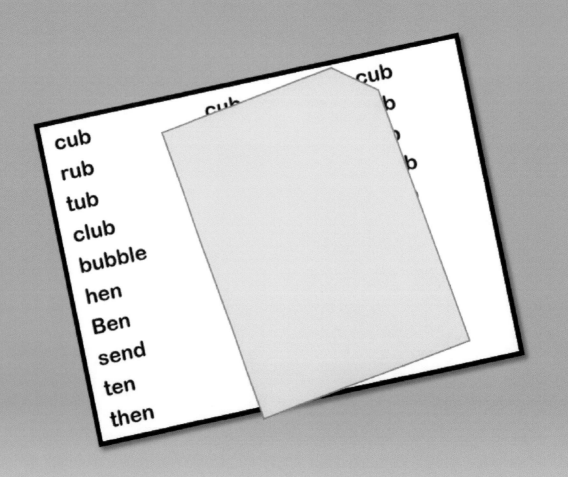

Jackson tried this and then Toby asked Jackson to spell them. Sure enough, Jackson knew them now. Jackson realised there was more to do before he could take Toby out into the garden. He had to tidy his room.

Jackson started to get his room tidied.

As he was putting things away, he noticed Toby copying him.

The two of them worked quickly together and soon the room was ready for Mum and Dad to inspect.

"Mum! Dad!" shouted Jackson. "Come and see!"

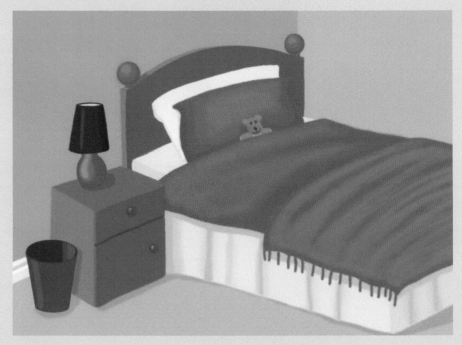

Mum and Dad were amazed at how tidy the room was. They were so pleased.

Dad asked Jackson his spellings to check his homework was done.

Mum was worried Jackson would not have learned his spellings. They were pleased he got them all right.

"Dad, Dad, can we go and play in the garden now"? asked Jackson.

Mum and Dad agreed that he could go out until it started to get dark.

Jackson and Toby ran out into the garden as quickly as they could.

The first thing Jackson wanted to do was to take Toby on a ride around the garden on his tractor and trailer.

Toby jumped up into the trailer
and away they went
around the garden.

Toby soon had enough fun going around in the trailer and so he jumped out.

Toby wanted to play a new game.

Toby suddenly disappeared and Jackson started to feel worried.

"Where did Toby go? He couldn't just disappear into thin air." thought Jackson.

Jackson quickly scanned the garden for Toby.

It didn't take Jackson long to spot two feet and a nose sticking out below one of the flower bushes.

Jackson tiptoed towards the bushes Toby was hiding under.

Jackson got a ball and started
to throw it for Toby to chase
and catch.

Toby loved to try and
catch the ball before
it hit the ground.

Toby was very good at catching the ball in flight.

They played ball until it was getting dark.

Then Jackson heard Dad calling them in.

Jackson took one more throw of the ball for Toby to chase, it was a big throw, so big the ball bounced too high for Toby to catch and it flew into the garden next door.

In next door's garden Toby was still sleeping and dreaming when suddenly he was hit with a ball.

Toby woke up and realized he had been dreaming about Jackson all along!

The End

LOCKDOWN *memories*

Toby finds a mask

BOOK-1

Written by David Bannister

Toby the Samoyed has various adventures. His first is finding a mask and discovering how to wear it.

A YEAR OF *adventures*

Toby the fire dog

BOOK-2

Written by David Bannister

His second adventure takes him into danger as he discovers a forest fire and rescues the day, becoming a hero.